ULTIMATE ADVENTURE SPORTS
SKYDIVING
- EXCLUSIVE -

AUTHOR
SALLY WARREN

Redback Publishing

PO Box 357, Frenchs Forest, NSW 2086, Australia

www.redbackpublishing.com
orders@redbackpublishing.com

© Redback Publishing 2023
ISBN 978-1-922322-96-8 HBK

All rights reserved. No part of this publication may be reproduced in any form or by any means (including photocopying or storing it in any medium by electronic means and whether or not transiently or incidentally to some other use of this publication) without the written permission of the copyright owner. Applications for the copyright owner's written permission should be addressed to the publisher.

Author: Sally Warren
Editor: Caroline Thomas
Designer: Redback Publishing

Original illustrations:
© Redback Publishing 2023
Originated by Redback Publishing

Printed and bound in Malaysia

Acknowledgements
Abbreviations: l—left, r—right, b—bottom, t—top,
c—centre, m—middle
We would like to thank the following for permission to reproduce photographs: (Images © Shutterstock) p1 Cam Puttee, p3mr Matt Laycock, p5m Jesse Warren, p7br Balon Greyjoy via Wikimedia, p7bl Red Bull Stratos via Flickr, p8t/br Kian Bullock, p10 Matt Laycock, p13tr/m/b Kian Bullock, p13bl Jesse Warren, p14t Jesse Warren, p17m Jesse Warren, p18 Cam Puttee, p20t Kian Bullock, p20m Yuri-D3/Shutterstock, p21t Opachevsky Irina/Shutterstock, p21br David Clarke, p22 Cam Puttee, p23br Cam Puttee, p24 Jules McConnell, p25tr Shital Mahajan-Rane, p25bl Felix Baumgartner, p25br Jeb Corliss, p26 by vivooo/Shutterstock, p27ml Tommy Larey/Shutterstock, p29t Kian Bullock, p29b Kian Bullock, p30t Juan Mayer, p30bl Gravity Indoor Skydiving, p30br Festivallyly via Wikimedia, p32 Kian Bullock.

Disclaimer
Every effort has been made to contact copyright holders of any material reproduced in this book. Any omissions will be rectified in subsequent printings if notice is given to the publisher.

A catalogue record for this book is available from the National Library of Australia

CONTENTS

What is Skydiving? **4**
Brief History **6**
Where do People Skydive? **8**
Learning to Skydive **10**
Disciplines Within the Sport **12**
What is a Canopy? **14**
What About Paragliding? **16**
Terminal Velocity **18**
Altitude **19**
Jump Aircraft **20**
Extra Equipment and Clothing **22**
Professional Skydiver Snapshots **24**
Indoor Skydiving **26**
Is Skydiving Safe? **28**
Skydiving Events **30**
Glossary **31**
Index **32**

EPIC ADVENTURE AWAITS!

WHAT IS SKYDIVING?

So you want to know about skydiving? Hold onto your hats and get ready to defy gravity!

Skydiving is the extreme sport of jumping out of an aeroplane and free-falling at a tremendous speed, through the sky.

There are two parts to a skydive:

FREE-FALLING

CANOPY RIDE

FREE-FALLING

Free-falling is the ultimate high! Once the plane gets to the right altitude, you gather your nerves and jump out. Free-fall is exhilarating and usually lasts around a minute depending on what height you jump from.

CANOPY RIDE

After having a wild ride in free-fall, canopy riding begins when you pull the parachute out of its bag. The parachute inflates and you fly through the clouds like a bird before landing safely on the ground.

BREAKING BARRIERS!

In 2012, Felix Baumgartner broke the 52-year record for the highest skydive by jumping from the edge of space! He travelled so fast that he broke the sound barrier!

BRIEF HISTORY

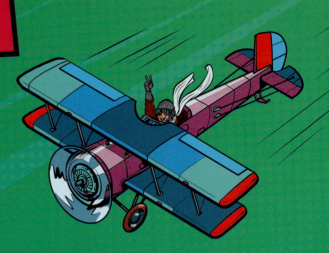

As early as medieval times, people performed skydiving stunts and aerial acrobatics. But while these new skills were thrilling, they were NOT always death-defying and too many people were either seriously injured or killed!

After aeroplanes were invented, scientists began performing experiments to make skydiving safer. Now, anyone can skydive, almost anywhere in the world. Awesome right?!

TIMELINE

12th Century
Evidence from China shows people used parachute-like devices to entertain guests at ceremonies

1483 Leonardo da Vinci sketched a man using a parachute, but no-one knows if the jump was ever made.

1919 Leslie Irvin recorded the first-ever recorded free-fall jump.

1939 By the end of World War II, military paratroopers had mastered the use of parachutes.

1960 Command Pilot, Colonel Joseph William Kittinger II, set the world record for the highest free-fall jump from a helium-balloon-tethered gondola, 31 kilometres above Earth.

2012 Felix Baumgartner smashed world records as the first human to break the sound barrier in free-fall at 1,357.6 km/h! Jumping from 39 kilometres above Earth, he also smashed Kittinger's 52-year record.

1952 After returning soldiers popularised the activity as a sport, skydiving soon became a national sport and competitions began.

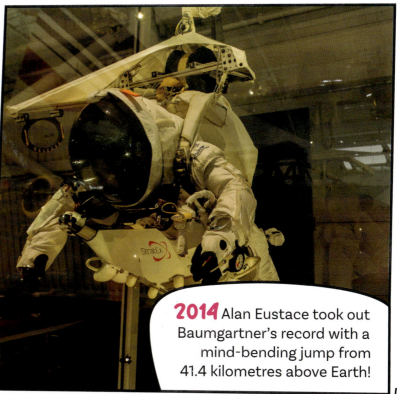

2014 Alan Eustace took out Baumgartner's record with a mind-bending jump from 41.4 kilometres above Earth!

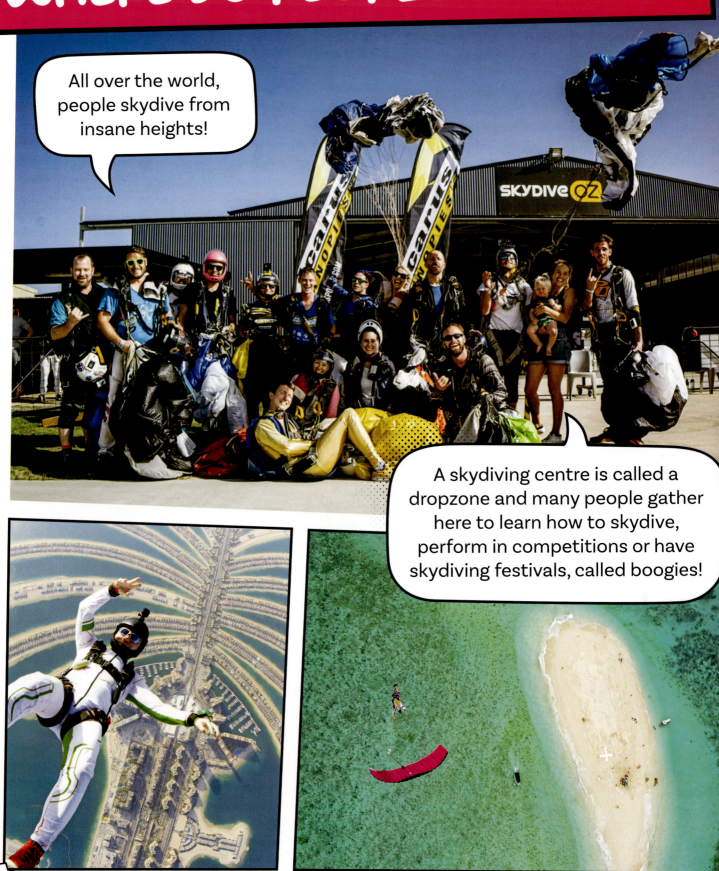

COOL STUFF

DIZZYING HEIGHTS!
You can skydive over Mount Everest at 23,000 feet (7,000 metres) from a helicopter - prices start at $22,000! (USD)

SOME OF THE CRAZIEST PLACES TO JUMP

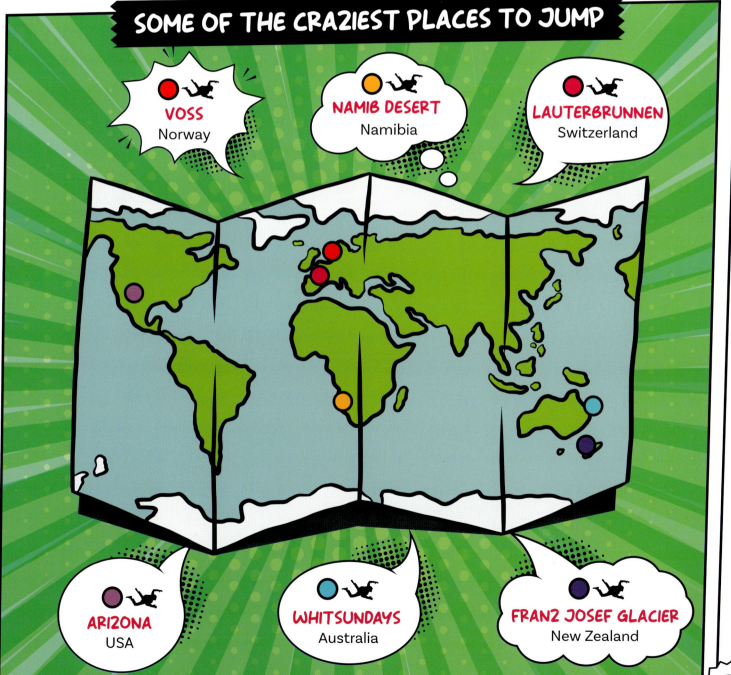

- **VOSS** — Norway
- **NAMIB DESERT** — Namibia
- **LAUTERBRUNNEN** — Switzerland
- **ARIZONA** — USA
- **WHITSUNDAYS** — Australia
- **FRANZ JOSEF GLACIER** — New Zealand

LEARNING TO SKYDIVE

You can skydive tandem without any qualifications, or you can take a giant leap and complete the AFF course. AFF stands for Accelerated Freefall and is a step-by-step course that teaches you all the skills to skydive solo. The AFF qualification is recognised all over the world.

A first skydive – make no mistake – is a very big life event!

HOW TO BECOME A FULLY QUALIFIED SKYDIVER

GROUND TRAINING

Before going up in the air, solo skydiving students need at least one full day of training down on the ground. You'll learn everything you need to know to do your first jump and, above all, you'll learn how to be safe.

3 - 2 - 1 - GO! On your first jump from a height, you will have an instructor on either side of you, holding onto your jumpsuit to keep you stable. After completing some skills in free-fall, you will open your parachute and the instructors will let go of you. But you're not completely alone! Skydivers wear headsets and communicate using radio. Combined with ground signals everyone can work together for a safe landing.

JUMPING WITH 2 INSTRUCTORS

After jumping with two instructors, you should be less nervous and more in control. Now it's time to just jump with one. Once they can see you are in control, they will let go of you and give you signals to do a mid-air 360 and even a backflip! Awesome!!

JUMPING WITH 1 INSTRUCTOR

JUMPING SOLO

After about nine or ten jumps you should be very proud! You will have completed your AFF course and are now allowed to jump solo!

DISCIPLINES WITHIN THE SPORT

"Who would have thought there were so many fun ways to fly through the sky?"

Jumping tandem is a great way for anyone to go skydiving. It's definitely less scary than a solo jump and can be a great once-in-a-lifetime experience! The passenger is attached to an instructor who controls the whole skydive, from exiting the plane to opening the parachute and flying it safely to the ground.

Licenced jumpers – with AFF qualifications – can go sport jumping! There are many different styles of sport jumping so you can get creative. Fly solo or fly with friends!

FORMATION SKYDIVING

WINGSUITING

ANGLE FLYING

CANOPY PILOTING

EPIC!

FREE FLYING

WHAT IS A CANOPY?

If you jump out of an aeroplane you're going to want to land safely on the ground without hitting it, right?

A canopy is the thing that saves your life and is otherwise known as a parachute. Canopies were once round and designed for a slow descent. Over time, the design became more elliptical, making the flight faster and giving the skydiver more control.

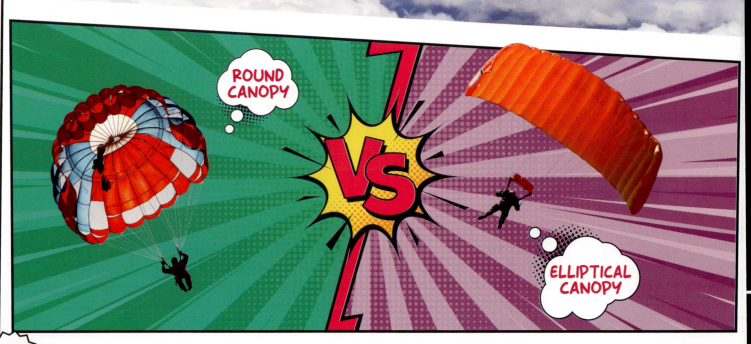

ROUND CANOPY VS ELLIPTICAL CANOPY

SUPER SAFE!

Skydivers make about 2 million jumps each year and less than one percent result in death. This makes skydiving safer than driving a car!

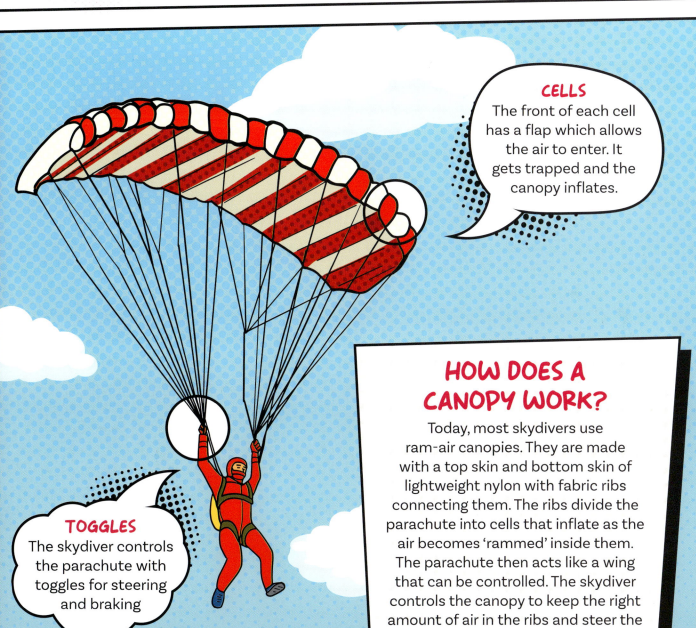

CELLS
The front of each cell has a flap which allows the air to enter. It gets trapped and the canopy inflates.

TOGGLES
The skydiver controls the parachute with toggles for steering and braking

HOW DOES A CANOPY WORK?

Today, most skydivers use ram-air canopies. They are made with a top skin and bottom skin of lightweight nylon with fabric ribs connecting them. The ribs divide the parachute into cells that inflate as the air becomes 'rammed' inside them. The parachute then acts like a wing that can be controlled. The skydiver controls the canopy to keep the right amount of air in the ribs and steer the dive safely to the drop zone.

WHAT ABOUT PARAGLIDING?

Looking for more extreme thrills? Paragliding is another adrenaline-pumping sport with the super thrill of human flight.

Unlike skydiving, there is no free-fall in paragliding. Starting with their wing on the ground, paragliders simply run off the edge of a hill! Sounds crazy, I know, but as you run the wing inflates and before you know it you're gliding through the air. Floating around in the sky and catching thermals is an amazing way to spend a day taking in the breathtaking views from above the clouds.

GEAR

A paragliding canopy is called a wing. It is larger than a skydiving wing but made of the same fabric. A paraglider wears a harness that allows them to sit back in comfort and fly for hours at a time!

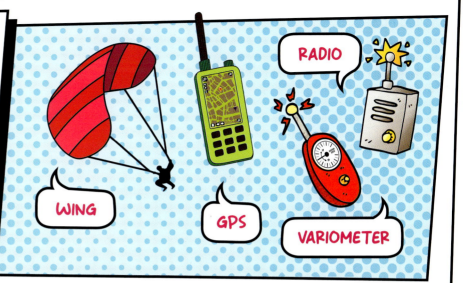

WING

GPS

RADIO

VARIOMETER

One very important skill that all paragliders learn before getting their licence, is the ability to read the weather. High winds and rain bombs are seriously no-fly days!

COOL STUFF

THREE AMIGOS

The world record for the longest paragliding flight is more than 11 hours. In that time, the three-man team covered over 588 kilometres.

TERMINAL VELOCITY

Just imagine stepping out of the plane into the wide-open sky! Insane right?

Free-falling is one of the most exciting thrills you can get. At first, you will fall faster and faster until you are no longer accelerating. This consistent falling speed is called terminal velocity. It happens when the downward force of gravity, matches the upward force of air resistance.

Most skydivers reach a terminal velocity of around 200 kilometres per hour in a belly-down position. But, changing position to a vertical and streamlined dive can increase this to around 804 kilometres per hour!

ALTITUDE

Altitude is a very important measure of the vertical distance of an object above sea level. A skydiver always needs to be aware of their altitude during free-fall, to know the right time to open the parachute and land safely.

ALTITUDE

Skydivers wear an altimeter on their wrist so they can check their height during the skydive.

COOL STUFF

DON'T SHOUT!
During a skydive, the wind passes past your ears so fast that it makes it impossible to hear a fellow skydiver.

JUMP AIRCRAFT

Who would jump out of a completely good aeroplane? A skydiver - that's who!

Not just any aeroplane, but one flown by a jump pilot who has done a special course and passed an exam to be allowed to carry skydivers to height. Each drop zone has different aeroplanes.

CESSNA 182

One of the most common but smallest skydiving planes is a Cessna 182. It can take four skydivers to an altitude of 3,000 metres in about 20 minutes. It's a bit squishy, but fun nevertheless! There is a small step and a strut you can hang onto as you exit the plane.

TWIN OTTER

The Twin Otter is a very popular twin-engine turbine jump plane. It's fast and can carry 22 skydivers to altitude in less than 15 minutes.

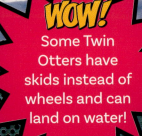

WOW! Some Twin Otters have skids instead of wheels and can land on water!

20

SKYVAN

By far, one of the most fun planes to jump out of is the skyvan. These big birds can carry 23 jumpers to height and the best bit is?

The tailgate door opens upward and you can run out the back with a big group of skydivers. Now that's totally epic!

KING AIR

Almost like a rocket ship to altitude, the King Air can take 15 skydivers to altitude in 10 minutes and is one of the fastest skydiving planes in the world!

EPIC! Check out the dive on this beast!

COOL STUFF

MAXIMUM FUN!

Some skydivers are lucky enough to fun jump from a helicopter or a hot air balloon!

21

EXTRA EQUIPMENT AND CLOTHING

> It takes passion, bravery and a willingness to step into the unknown when you decide to become a skydiver... But without the proper gear, you won't get very far!

SKYDIVING PARACHUTE
This is absolutely the most important piece of gear you need. New skydivers start out with a bigger parachute that makes descent slower. With experience, skydivers downsize into something smaller and faster.

All skydiving rigs contain two parachutes. The first is called a main and the second is only used for backup. This is called a reserve.

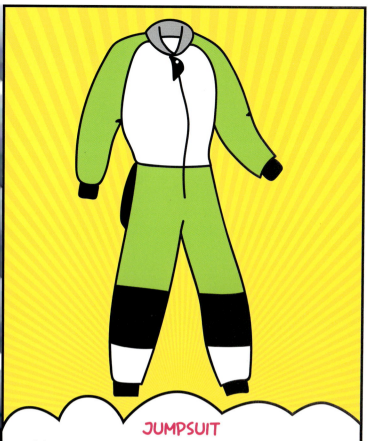

JUMPSUIT
Hold up – you want to look cool right? A jumpsuit will not only make you look good but will help with your flying skills too. There are different suits for different disciplines and each has special features. Some are tight and others are baggy. Some even have built-in wings!

SKYDIVING AAD
An AAD is a real-life lifesaver! It stands for Automatic Activation Device and is installed inside your rig. An AAD will deploy your reserve parachute if you don't get to your main in time.

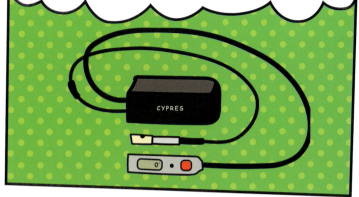

ALTIMETER
An altimeter will tell you what height you're at. It is usually worn on the wrist and looks like a big watch. Some are digital and others are analogue but having one is very important – not only for free-fall but also for your landing, so you know when to turn.

HELMET
Although a helmet is not compulsory at some drop zones, it is a good idea to wear one anyway. It will protect you during exit, free-fall and landing. It's also a great way to cover your hair – free-fall tangles are out of control!

PROFESSIONAL SKYDIVERS

JULES MCCONNELL
BORN: 19.07.1976

Jules McConnel is Australian born, has been jumping for 26 years and has done over 11,000 skydives. She is most famous for her part in the 100-way canopy formation world record and holds the Australian record of 150 jumps in a single day! Jules jumps, coaches, competes, juggles and paraglides – is there anything this woman can't do?

SHITAL MAHAJAN-RANE

BORN: 19.09.1982

Indian extreme sportswoman and total badass, Shital Mahajan Rane, is the holder of eight world records. She is the first person to skydive over Antarctica and the youngest woman to jump over both the North and the South Poles.

JEB CORLISS

BORN: 25.03.1976

Jeb Corliss is an American professional skydiver and BASE jumper. He is most famous for jumping off structures such as the Eiffel Tower and Brazil's Christ the Redeemer. His famous wingsuit jump in China, called the 'flying dagger', saw him fly through a crack only 18 metres wide at the top and less than five metres across the bottom!

FELIX BAUMGARTNER

BORN: 20.04.1969

Felix Baumgartner is an Austrian skydiver best known for his record-breaking stratosphere jump to Earth from a helium balloon in 2012. He is also a BASE jumper, adventurous daredevil and part of the Red Bull team of athletes.

INDOOR SKYDIVING

Say What?! You can actually fly indoors?

Believe it or not, indoor skydiving facilities are amazing fun! They are called wind tunnels and anyone can fly there, from ages 3 to 103. Some people use them for fun but skydivers use them to train for competitions and also to fast-track their skill in a controlled environment.

BEWARE! Indoor skydiving is highly addictive. Sometimes you can have too much fun!

HOW DOES IT WORK?
Really powerful fans direct a continuous stream of air upwards, into a vertical cylinder. At about 200 kilometres an hour, this re-creates the air resistance in a natural free-fall.

CYLINDER

NET

BIG FAN

SPACE AGE!
The first wind tunnel was built by NASA in the 1940s, but it wasn't powerful enough for human flight. In 1964, a stronger one was built at the Wright-Patterson airbase in the USA. It was here that Jack Tiffany became the first recorded human to ever fly indoors in a wind tunnel.

IS SKYDIVING SAFE?

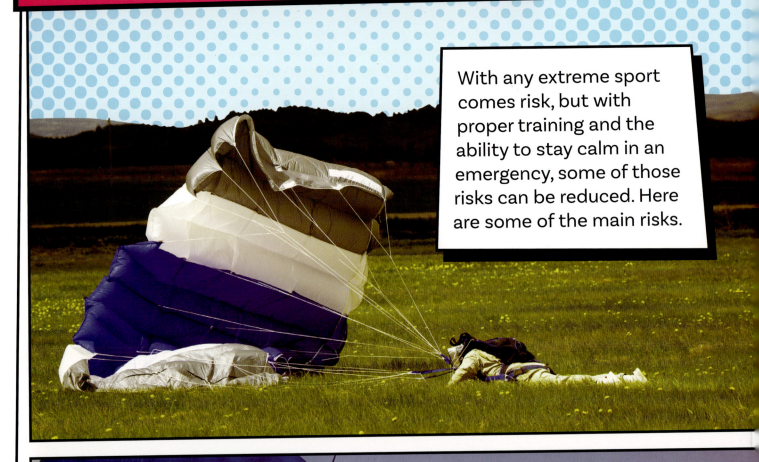

With any extreme sport comes risk, but with proper training and the ability to stay calm in an emergency, some of those risks can be reduced. Here are some of the main risks.

MALFUNCTIONS

Parachute malfunctions can happen when you deploy your parachute. This means that sometimes something goes wrong and the parachute doesn't open properly. This happens in around one in every 1,000 jumps.

INJURY ON LANDING

Landing a parachute takes huge focus and concentration and it's important to have a solid landing plan. If something small happens and you forget to pull the brakes on your canopy at the right time or get simply distracted you can very easily hurt yourself.

INJURY DURING FREE-FALL

In free-fall skydivers travel at speeds of around 200 kilometres per hour. If they hit someone or something, it will hurt. A lot! Sometimes, this can result in injuries and even death.

SKYDIVING EVENTS

There are events held all over the world for skydivers to have fun, compete and learn new skills. Each drop zone has their own calendar of events and a great community of welcoming thrill-seekers.

Some of the most important competitions held include:

SKYDIVING WORLD CUP

SWOOP WORLD CUP

INDOOR SKYDIVING CHAMPIONSHIPS

GLOSSARY

AAD	Automatic Activation Device
AFF COURSE	Accelerated Freefall training and eventual qualification
ALTIMETER	wrist-worn device that displays altitude
ALTITUDE	height of an object above sea level
ANALOGUE	non-digital devices that can include watches and altimeters
ANGLE FLYING	flying at an angle, usually to steer towards other people during flight
BOOGIE	skydiving festival where people come together to do lots of skydiving
CANOPY	parachute or wing that slows and controls a skydiver's descent
DEPLOY	put an object into use
DROPZONE	landing and gathering area for skydivers
FORMATION SKYDIVING	groups of skydivers who create formations of people in mid-air
FREE-FALL	falling without a parachute yet deployed
FREEFLYING	skydiving with alternative body positions that are not 'belly-to-Earth'
GPS	Global Positioning System
GRAVITY	force that acts on objects to pull them towards Earth
MALFUNCTION	problem in the way that something works
NYLON	lightweight and flexible material made from plastics
PARACHUTE	device for catching air to create resistance that slows a falling object
PARAGLIDING	flying using a parachute after a running take-off from a cliff or hill
PARATROOPERS	soldiers who skydive into battle
RAM-AIR CANOPY	self-inflating parachute with two layers of fabric held together by ribs
SOUND BARRIER	increase in air resistance on an object travelling at the speed of sound
SWOOP	to skim near to the ground or water in a fast forward motion
TANDEM	two people doing something together
TERMINAL VELOCITY	where acceleration stops due to a balance between air resistance and drag force
VARIOMETER	device that measures the rate of descent using air pressure at altitude
WIND TUNNEL	man-made tunnel to channel air, as a high-speed wind simulation
WING	canopy or parachute used for flying
WINGSUITING	skydiving while wearing a suit with webbed arms and legs, to increase glide and flight time

INDEX

AEROPLANE	20, 21
ALTITUDE	4, 19-21, 30
ANGLE FLYING	13, 30
BAUMGARTNER	5, 7, 24
CANOPY	13-15, 17, 24, 28, 30
FREE-FALL	4, 5, 7, 10, 16, 18, 19, 23, 26, 27, 30
FORMATION SKYDIVING	13, 24, 30
GRAVITY	4, 18, 30
PARACHUTE	5, 7, 10, 12, 14, 15, 19, 22, 27, 28, 30
PARAGLIDING	16, 17, 24, 30
SOLO	10-12
SOUND BARRIER	5, 7, 30
SPORT JUMPING	12, 13
TERMINAL VELOCITY	18, 30
WINGSUITING	13, 25, 30

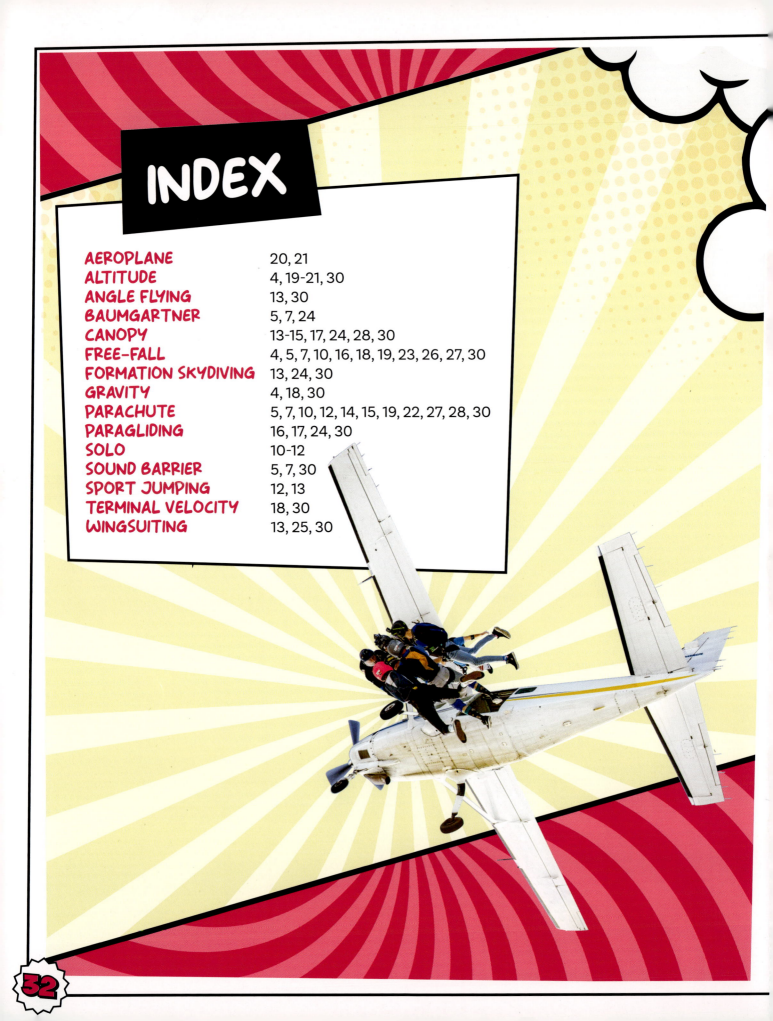